Sit Down, Shut Up & Hang On!

Sit Down, Shut Up & Hang On!

A BIKER'S GUIDE TO LIFE

Penny Powers & Chuck Hays

Illustrated by Anne Mitchell

GIBBS·SMITH
P
PUBLISHER

SALT LAKE CITY

03 02 01 00 5 4 3 2

Published by
Gibbs Smith, Publisher
P.O. Box 667
Layton, UT 84041

Design by Anne Mitchell
Manufactured in the U.S.A.

Library of Congress Cataloging-in-Publication Data
Powers, Penny, 1948-
Sit down, shut up and hang on: a bikers guide to life / text,
Penny Powers and Chuck Hays; illustrations, Anne
Mitchell.---1st ed.
p. cm.
ISBN 0-87905-781-5
1. Motorcycling-Anecdotes. 2. Motorcyclists-Anecdotes.
I.Hays, Chuck, 1961 -. II. Title.
GV1059.5.H39 1996
796.7'5-dc20   96-41583
                                                         CIP

*To those
who have ridden
these roads before,
thank you.*

Midnight bugs taste best.

Saddlebags can never hold everything you want, but they can hold everything you need.

*Wear
heavy boots.*

*You can't
kick things when
you're wearing
sneakers.*

*Never argue
with a woman holdin'
a torque wrench.*

If you're a complainer, ride at the back of the pack so you won't contaminate the rest of the group.

Never try to race an
OLD GEEZER—
he may have one more
gear than you.

The size of the
PISTON
don't tell you
nothin' about the
DEPTH
of the stroke.

Home
is where your bike
sits still long enough
to leave a few drops of
oil on the ground.

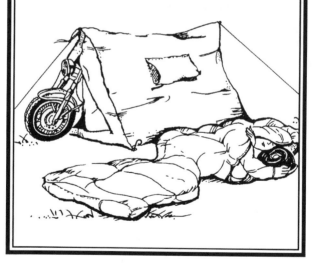

You'll get farther down the road if you learn to use more than two fingers on the front brake.

Routine maintenance should never be neglected.

It takes more love to share the saddle than it does to share the bed.

The only good view of a thunderstorm is in your rearview mirror.

OBJECTS IN MIRROR ARE CLOSER
THAN THEY APPEAR

Never
be afraid to
slow down.

*O*nly bikers understand
why dogs love to stick
their heads out
car windows.

Bikes
don't leak oil,
they mark their
territory.

Never ask a biker for directions if you're in a hurry to get there.

If it takes more than three bolts to hold it on, it's probably crucial.

Anything that shows up on more than two bikes is a FAD.

Remember that you will be judged by the horse you rode in on.

Don't ride so late into the night that you sleep through the sunrise.

*Pie and coffee
are as important
as gasoline.*

CUBIC INCHES
is what it's
all about.

*Remember
your mistakes
as well as
your triumphs.*

Don't
sleep where your foot can hit the kickstand.

Drink Hard, Ride Fast, Die Young.

When people think you're a rude, crude, scum-sucking cretin, they generally don't ask you stupid questions.

*I*t don't take
muscle to ride, but
it takes grace
to ride well.

There's more to riding a motorcycle than holdin' on to the handlebars and keepin' yer feet on the pegs.

Despite everything else, there's still some kind of kinship between a real badass biker and a cop on a hog.

Don't mess with the locals.

All motorcycles
have personalities.

Some are
gold-digging harlots.

Some are
homicidal maniacs.

It's a good thing they make so many different kinds of motorcycles, 'cause no two people can agree on which one's the best.

"*Bigger*" don't always mean "*more powerful.*"

The number of kicks it takes to start your bike is directly proportional to the number of spectators.

***Never ask
your bike to
scream before her
throat is good
and warm.***

Sometimes it takes a whole tankful of gas before you can think straight.

If you want to get a job, you may have to compromise your principles.

You may even have to shave.

*R*iding faster than everyone else only guarantees you'll ride alone.

*Never hesitate
to ride past the last
streetlight at the
edge of town.*

Never *mistake horsepower* *for staying power.*

A
good rider has balance, judgement, and timing.

So does a good lover.

A cold hamburger can be reheated quite nicely by strapping it to an exhaust pipe and riding forty miles.

Never
do less than
forty miles before
breakfast.

If you don't ride in the rain—you don't ride.

A bike
on the road
is worth two in
the shop.

Respect the person who has seen the dark side of motorcycling— and lived.

*Young riders
pick a destination
and go.*

*Old riders
pick a direction
and go.*

Overconfidence can be supplied by spare spark plugs, a set of wrenches, and a roll of toilet paper.

Never
offer to fight an
OLD GEEZER.

IF YOU WIN—
there's no glory.

IF YOU LOSE—
your reputation
is shot.

A good "wrench"
will let you watch
without charging you
for it.

Advice
is free and worth
every penny.

Sometimes the fastest way to get there is to stop for the night.

Always
back your scoot
into the curb—
and sit where you
can see it.

Running late? Remember, motorcycles can split lanes.

Whatever it is, it's better done in the wind.

TWO-LANE BLACKTOP ISN'T A HIGHWAY— IT'S AN ATTITUDE

When you look down the road, it seems to never end— but you better believe it does.

***Winter*
*is Nature's way
of telling you
to polish.***

A
motorcycle can't sing on the streets of a city.

Keep
your bike
in good repair:
motorcycle boots
are not comfortable
for walking.

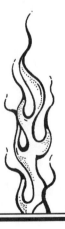

People are like motorcycles: each one is customized a bit differently.

More races were won in the tavern than on the track.

Never *loan your bike* *to someone else,* *and never ride* *another's.*

If the bike ain't braking properly, you don't start by rebuilding the engine.

Motorcycling
is a giant game of
**"MINE'S
BIGGER THAN
YOURS."**

Remember *to pay as much attention to your partner as you do your carburetor.*

Sometimes the best communication happens when you're on separate bikes.

Well-trained reflexes are quicker than luck.

*Good coffee
should be
indistinguishable
from 50-weight oil.*

The best alarm clock is sunshine on chrome.

Learn to do counterintuitive things that may someday save your butt.

*The twisties—
not the superslabs—
separate the bikers
from the squids.*

Beware the biker
whose ink peels off.

New leather
don't smell right.

When you're riding lead, don't spit.

If you really want to know what's going on, watch what's happening at least five cars ahead.

Don't make a reputation you'll have to live down or run away from later.

If the person in the next lane at the stoplight rolls up the window and locks the door, support their view of life by snarling at them.

*S*moke and grease
can hide a
multitude of errors,
but only for so long.

A friend is someone who'll get out of bed at 2 A.M. to drive his pickup to the middle of nowhere to get you when you're broken down.

If she changes her oil more often than she changes her mind— follow her.

*The thicker
your oil,
the hotter you
can take it.*

Catchin' a June bug at 70 mph can double your vocabulary.

*I*f you want
to get somewhere
before sundown,
you can't stop at
every tavern.

There's somethin' ugly about the sight of a new bike on a trailer.

You can always hear a classic open primary— it sounds like $1.34 in change is loose in the friction plates.

Hunger can make even roadkill taste good.

You gotta be smart enough to understand the rules of motorcycling, and dumb enough to think the game's important.

Don't lead the pack if you don't know where you're goin'.

If you leave without one of your group, you better hope he doesn't catch up at the next stop.

Sleep with one arm through the spokes and keep your pants on.

Practice
wrenching
on your own
bike.

Everyone crashes.
Some get back on.
Some don't.
Some can't.

Three things can't be trusted: a fart, a cook, and a rearview mirror.

BEWARE
the biker who
says the bike never
breaks down.

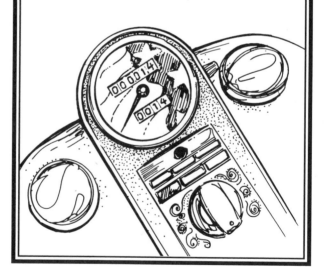

Some bikes run on 99-octane ego.

***O**wning two bikes is useful because at least one can be raided for parts at any given time.*

You'll know she loves you if she offers to let you ride her bike. Don't do it and she'll love you even more.

Don't argue with an eighteen wheeler.

Don't lean on the horn
'til you're out of danger.
Then blast it for all
you're worth.

**Never
be ashamed to
unlearn an
old habit.**

Maintenance is as much art as it is science.

A good long ride can clear your mind, restore your faith, and use up a lot of gasoline.

If the countryside seems boring, stop, get off your bike, and go sit in the ditch long enough to appreciate what was here before the asphalt came.

If you can't get it goin' with bungee cords and electrician's tape—it's serious.

If you ride like there's no tomorrow—there won't be.

*B*ikes parked out front mean good chicken-fried steak inside.

If you want to complain about the pace being set by the road captain, you better be prepared to lead the group yourself.

Gray-haired bikers don't get that way from pure luck.

*There are
drunk bikers.*

*There are
old bikers.*

*There are no old,
drunk bikers.*

We don't
need no steenkin'
weekend warriors.

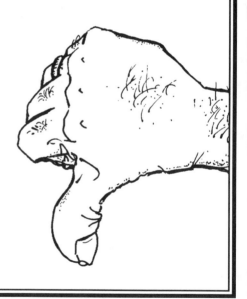

*Thin leather
looks good in the bar,
but it won't save
you from "road rash"
if you go down.*

The best modifications cannot be seen from the outside.

Always replace the cheapest parts first.

You can forget what you do for a livin' when your knees are in the breeze.

No matter what marque you ride, it's all the same wind.

It takes both pistons and cylinders to make a bike run.

One is not more important than the other.